To My Daughter

When you read this
Look you will realize
how precious you are to me.
How much I love you.
Someday please pass this
Look to your daughter. Kisses

Look With love Mom 1998 (Dec)

My Daughter, my joy...

First published simultaneously in 1998 by Exley Publications Ltd in Great Britain,
and Exley Publications LLC in the USA.
This edition published in North America by Books Are Fun, Ltd. in 1998.

12 11 10 9 8 7 6 5 4 3 2 1

ISBN 1-58209-006-8

Words and pictures selected by Helen Exley.
Pictures researched by Image Select International.
Printed in Singapore.

"My Daughter, my joy..." is dedicated to my dear mother Momtom.
As I conceived, and researched, and read, and moulded, and re-read, and
checked this book, I was constantly aware of the great love
and generosity she's given to me. Thank you for everything, Helen.

EXLEY
NEW YORK • WATFORD, UK

My Daughter, my joy...

THE GREATEST TRIBUTES TO DAUGHTERS THAT HAVE EVER BEEN WRITTEN

A HELEN EXLEY GIFTBOOK

the nicest things

that happen to people

Little girls are the nicest things that happen to people.

They are born with a little bit of angelshine about them,

and though it wears thin sometimes

there is always enough left to lasso your heart —

even when they are sitting in the mud,

or crying temperamental tears,

or parading up the street in mother's best clothes.

ALAN BECK

Small child. Clear crystal.

Bright and clear.

Faceted as none before you.

Catching the light from every lovely thing

and turning it to rainbow.

Reflecting beauty back into the world.

Making all things new.

reflecting beauty

PAMELA DUGDALE

the world is

Daughters are sudden ecstatic smiles, funny walks, and puzzlements. They are blown kisses, cuddles, gifts and daisies, strokings of stockings, pattings of hands, the offerings of help in pouring concrete, electrical repairs and the icing of a cake.

No one is so astonished, so appalled, so easily impressed. No one responds with so complete a rapture to one's offerings of farmyard imitations, or small surprises.

For them the world is full of marvels that they long to share with you — pointing with eager fingers to blossoming trees and rainbow puddles, robins on the lawn, a man up a ladder, a woman in a flagrant hat.

... .And if there are times when they wail in the library or clamp their lips together when confronted with a spoon — it will pass.

CHARLOTTE GRAY, b.1937

full of marvels

I snuggle close to my daughter before she is awake,
feel her warm, peaceful breathing, and hope
that through her I may become what
I wished to be.

LIV ULLMANN, FROM "CHANGING"

Spring, the birth of nature; soft air filled

with the promise of warmth, sun speckling

the ground and a new young mother with

her baby daughter soothed and asleep in

her arms under a tree.

What nicer piece of life?

JANE–LOUISE MIDDLETON

"Thank heavens for little girls." And they are not just their potential as women. With pigtails and pony tails, in jeans and party dresses, climbing trees, reading books, sucking gobstoppers and turning cartwheels, making friends and breaking friends, they bring their special charm into the world, a delight in detail, a tenderness in relationship, a sensitivity to joy and sorrow and spiritual truth; the many attributes which make them different from little boys.

MICHELE GUINNESS,
FROM "TAPESTRY OF VOICES"

they bring their
special charm

Your pain

I could not bear for you.

I could not remember

my pain for you.

Only the small life in my arms —

My girl, my daughter — you.

BARBARA RENNIE

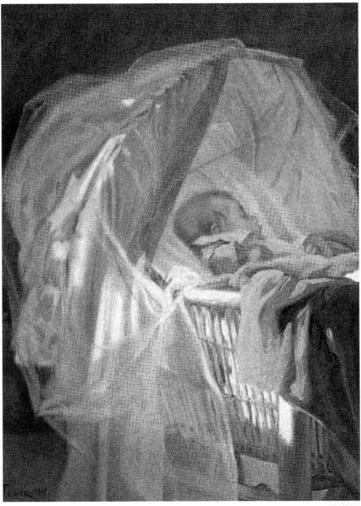

for you my

NAVAJO CHANT

I have made a baby board for you my daughter

May you grow to a great old age

Of the sun's rays I have made the back

Of black clouds I have made the blanket

Of rainbow I have made the bow

Of sunbeams I have made the side loops

Of lightning I have made the lacings

Of raindrops have I made the footboard,

Of dawn have I made the bed covering....

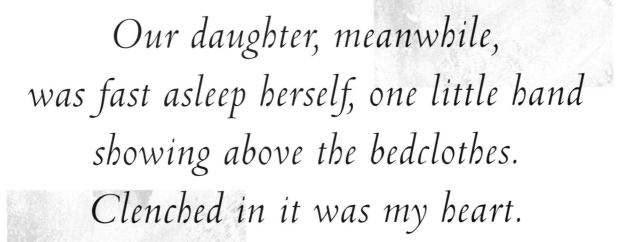

I creep into her room and stare down at her.

Smooth baby skin, beautiful sleeping face and soft,

downy fair hair. I'd rather look than pick her up,

my brand new daughter — I'm still scared

I'll harm her with my awkwardness.

NICOLE SWAIN

Our daughter, meanwhile,
was fast asleep herself, one little hand
showing above the bedclothes.
Clenched in it was my heart.

HUGO WILLIAMS,
b. 1942,
FROM "WHAT SHALL WE DO NOW THAT WE HAVE DONE EVERYTHING"

the

that

a

ONE OF THE IRONIES OF BEING A PARENT

IS THAT YOU HAVE YOUR CHILDREN

A LIMITED NUMBER OF YEARS,

AND YOU SELDOM SEE THEM. YOU MAY SELDOM

HEAR FROM THEM. BUT THE POWER

A CHILD HAS OVER YOU LASTS A LIFETIME.

BETTE DAVIS, FROM "THIS 'N THAT"

The whisper of a baby girl

can be heard further

than the roar of a lion.

ARAB PROVERB

But for those moments, as the doctor

shoved cotton wool up your flat nose

and swabbed your eyes and cleaned your bum

I forgot completely all my life and love

and watched you like a pool of growing light

and whispered to myself "She's come! She's come!"

BRIAN JONES

Then they handed her to me,

stiff and howling,

and I held her for the first time

and kissed her,

and she went still and quiet

as though by instinctive guile,

and I was instantly enslaved

by her flattery of my powers.

LAURIE LEE (1914-1997), FROM "TWO WOMEN"

A daughter. An astonishment. A perfection.
The newest thing in the world. So small.
So packed with secrets.
And every day brings fresh wonders — for every smile,
every gesture is an enchantment. Everything is unexpected.
(Quick! — see what she's doing now!)
Her face lights up when you — most ordinary you —
come into sight. Your songs delight her.
You are the one who can soothe her into sleep,
drive off her terrors, lever her from tears to laughter.
She is so beautiful, so funny, so eager, so resolute.
And she loves you with all her heart.
No one has failed who has so dear a daughter.

PAM BROWN, b.1928

your life was changed

The baby was born and your life was changed more than you ever dreamed.

You found you had sprouted invisible antennae that picked up every alteration

in breathing, every variation in temperature, every nuance of expression

in your tiny daughter. No one told you that the change was irreversible.

That you would feel in your own heart every pain, every loss, every

disappointment, every rebuff, every cruelty that she experiences — life long.

ROSANNE AMBROSE-BROWN, b. 1943

Emily is wonderful:
she's like the sun,
she comes out and everyone
starts feeling warmer.

JILLY COOPER

They have what no grown up has – that directness – chatter, chatter, chatter,

on Ann goes, in a kind of world of her own, with its seals and dogs; happy

because she's going to have cocoa tonight, and go blackberrying tomorrow.

The walls of her mind are all hung round with such bright vivid things,

and she doesn't see what we see.

VIRGINIA WOOLF (1882-1941),

FROM "A WRITER'S DIARY"

she's

like the sun

he grows
with her,
learning
as they
go

He grows with his first daughter, learning as they go. He feels with her — each restlessness, each fear, each pain. She laughs and he is overjoyed. She reaches out her little arms to him and he rejoices.

She sleeps on his shoulder and he does not move, for fear of waking her. He shows her marvels and lives her astonishment in bird and cat and falling leaf. He asks for kisses. Hugs. The invisible gifts that she bestows on those she loves — held carefully between minute thumb and finger.

He fields her as she falls. Wraps her against the cold. Dries her from her bath. Boasts casually to friends of her achievements. Hoards photographs in case he should forget.

All disappointments, all failures, fade like mist before this golden girl. His daughter.

PAM BROWN, b. 1928

Once I picked up Lia at Brownie camp. She was six years old and came running out to the car in her new khaki uniform with an orange bandana around her neck and a little beanie on her head. She had just made it into the Potawatami Tribe. She had hoped to join the Nava-joes, as she called them, but she was turned down. Still, she was excited, and so was I. Funny thing, I missed an important meeting that day, but for the life of me I have no recollection of what it was.

LEE IACOCCA, b.1924

better

Daughters do wonderful things.

Not the wonderful things you expected them to do.

Different things.

Astonishing things.

Better than you ever dreamed.

MARION C. GARRETTY, b. 1917

than you ever

dreamed

... in that moment of my desperation she let fly her first real smile: not a shy, average, half-moon smile — but an open-mouthed, toothless, silly wide gas of delight. She chortled at me, and despite my stupor, I laughed back. She'd taken me by surprise, and exhaustion dropped away, flooded out on waves of pure maternal bliss. Later, when she was finally asleep again, I'd tried to sketch our exchange. Her smile had matured and her teeth had come in, but the spirit — that wild sense of humour — had been Anna and stayed Anna from that minute on.

Now I put my finger into her palm and she curled her fingers around mine, opened her eyes, saw me watching. I had wanted her to wake up, I realized, to see her smile again. One grin, sleepily, then she turned her face back into the pillow.

LINDA GRAY SEXTON

The baby has learned to smile, and her smiles burst forth like
holiday sparklers, lighting our hearts. Joy fills the room.
At what are we smiling? We don't know, and we don't care.
We are communicating with one another in happiness,
and the smiles are the outward display of our delight and our love.

JOAN LOWERY NIXON

*V*ery gingerly, holding my breath, I rested my hand on the side, and stretched out two of my fingers, to take gently hold of Imogen's hand. It felt so soft I could scarcely register the touch on my skin, so warm and light. It was like the paw of a baby dormouse I once found in the garden, but that had been cold, the dormouse dead. My baby daughter was alive! I stroked her hand with my finger – and then put it into her palm. At once she gripped me, so tightly I was startled. And then, looking at her, feeling her minute pink fingers holding so hard to mine, I was hit sideways and bowled over by a great rush of love – the purest, tenderest, most passionately committed love I have ever felt for anyone or anything in my life. I think I will never experience it again, it was as pure as pure oxygen, pure alcohol, fierce, heady, undiluted, strong.

"Oh little one, *live – live!*" I cried to her, silently.

SUSAN HILL, b. 1942,
FROM "FAMILY"

*She looked up at me.
The crying stopped.
Her eyes melted
through me,
forging a connection
in me with
their soft heat.*

SHIRLEY MACLAINE

HAVING A CHILD ALTERS

THE RIGHTS OF EVERY MAN,

AND I DON'T EXPECT TO LIVE

AS I DID WITHOUT HER.

I AM HERS TO BE WITH,

AND HOPE TO BE WHAT SHE NEEDS,

AND KNOW OF NO REASON WHY

I SHOULD EVER DESERT HER.

LAURIE LEE

(1 9 1 4 - 1 9 9 7)

SOMEONE'S FACE

Someone's face was all frowned shut,
All squeezed full of grims and crinkles,
Pouts and scowls and gloomers, but
I could see behind the wrinkles —

Even with her face a-twist,
I saw Someone peeking through.
And when Someone's nose was kissed,
Guess who came out giggling — YOU!

JOHN CIARDI

THERE WAS A LITTLE GIRL

There was a little girl,
Who had a little curl
Right in the middle of her forehead;
And when she was good
She was very, very good,
But when she was bad she was horrid.

HENRY WADSWORTH LONGFELLOW
(1807-1882)

When you are a father, and you hear your children's voices,

you will feel that those little ones are akin to every drop in your

veins; that they are the very flower of your life and you will

cleave so closely to them that you seem to feel every movement

that they make.

HONORE DE BALZAC (1799-1850), FROM "LE PERE GORIOT"

I love my little girl an extraordinary amount; I have,
in fact, surprised myself with my talent for fathering.
Since her birth I have been so wholly preoccupied with
the minutiae of her progress — from the growth of the
microscopic hairs on her bald head to the lengthening of
her attention span — that I have been effectively lost to
the larger world.

HARRY STEIN

There is something infinitely precious about having a daughter. Mine, from the moment she was born, drew from me reserves of tenderness, protectiveness and fight I never knew I possessed. I wanted to change the world overnight, to make it a safer, easier, better place for this miniature woman, this receptacle of all my dreams and aspirations, this extension of myself.

MICHELE GUINNESS, FROM "TAPESTRY OF VOICES"

She held my attention like a fiery constellation. Her eyes bewitched me. Her first smile caused me and Jon to waltz around the room with the baby between us. We were besotted with her, the first parents in history.

ERICA JONG, b. 1942, FROM "FEAR OF FIFTY"

You will never be free again.
You live two lives now, hers and your own.
And the greatest pain is having to let her
make her own choices —
whatever your experience foretells.
Mercifully, this life link carries happiness
as well as heartache.
You are allowed to touch her joys,
to share the triumphs and excitements.
Distance cannot divide you.
There will be nights without sleep.
Days of waiting for a word. But letters.
Unexpected phone calls.
The astonishment of her standing on the doorstep
when you thought her half a world away.
And happiness beyond anything
you ever thought possible. Surprises. Amazement.
For she is your diamond daughter.
She can cut across your heart and mind.

ROSANNE AMBROSE-BROWN, b.1943

protection and

Father and daughter. It is a magic

relationship. It softens strong,

uncommunicative men. It provides

protection and strength for the young girl.

It is a fundamental bond to both people.

Every father who has held his daughter

close, and felt the shudder of her touch, is

affected for life. Any daughter who has felt

deeply loved and harbored by her father, also

carries that with her for life.

HELEN THOMSON, b. 1943

*I*t was one of those days. Everything had gone wrong.
I was run ragged. House, husband, children — it all seemed
too much. Near to tears I heard myself blurting, "I want my
mummy." I didn't expect an answer — but I got one.
There was a scamper and a breathless, "Don't worry.
I'll be your mummy." It was my four-year-old daughter
Grace — and the expression on her face as she threw back her head
and smiled up at me was beautiful to see.
My own very personal sun began to shine again — brilliantly.
And it has been shining ever since. Grace has seen to that.
Married now and with children of her own, she still finds time
to "mother" me. There is still that same beautiful long-ago smile.
Grace tells me — God bless her! — I was a wonderful mother.
I know one thing. I have a wonderful daughter.

J.B. GRIFFITHS,
IN A LETTER ABOUT HER DAUGHTER

"I'll be your mummy"

Your first butterfly.

Your first rainbow.

Your first dinosaur.

Thank you for

the chance to

rediscover the world.

PAMELA DUGDALE

... when she cried her deep soulful cry, I was filled not merely with panic

but with passion. I loved her even more for not being beautiful.

But was she comfortable? Were those sunbeams perhaps a little too strong?

Did they cause her a moment's inconvenience? I would smash the sun

to smithereens if they did. It would be the work of a moment: nothing easier.

I would weep tears of anguish the while. There seemed to be lots of

anguish about. I only had to imagine her suffering anything at the hands

of anybody and I sprouted claws and fangs. I would tear her assailants

limb from limb. Motherhood seemed to have turned me,

overnight, into a sabre-toothed tiger.

SUE LIMB, FROM "LOVE FORTY"

cried

cry

I wrapped you in protection, yet each time telling myself

"teach her to clad herself in armor and be brave.

I must remember to love her enough to let her fall."

DONNA GREEN

I wish I could save you from anxiety and sorrow. But then — how pink and fluffy and monotonous your life would be! So I wish for you courage and clear thinking, hope and a happy heart. Always.

PAMELA DUGDALE

for you courage

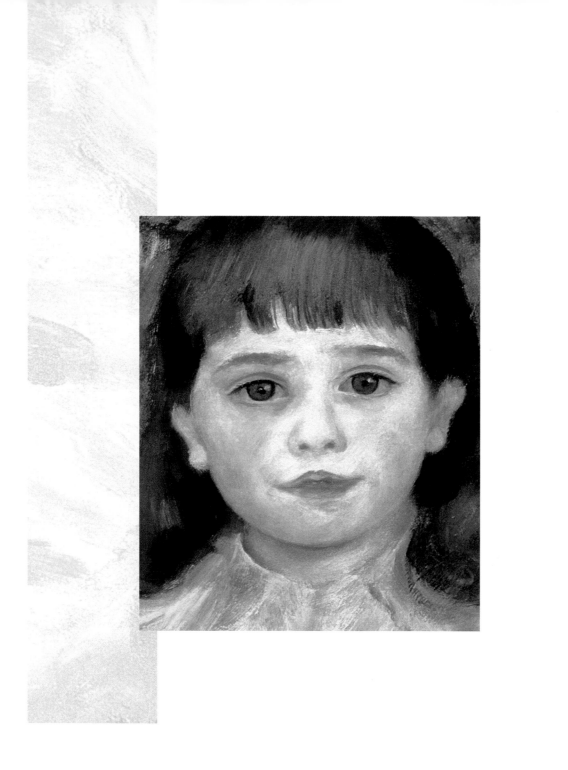

*J*osephine, when she was five or six years old, lightened my heart one evening when she flung her arms around me and said, "Oh, Mama, you're so exciting!" What more glorious compliment could a child give a parent? My parents were exciting to me, but their lives were far more glamorous than mine. When Jo made that lovely, spontaneous remark I felt anything but exciting; I was in the midst of a difficult decade of literary rejection, of struggling with small children and a large house; and that remark of Jo's restored my faith in myself, both as a writer and as a mother.

Even though I knew I might never again be published, even though I could not see any end to the physical struggle and perpetual fatigue, Josephine helped heal doubt. It is a risky business to hope, but my daughter gave me the courage to take the risk.

MADELEINE L'ENGLE,
FROM "THE SUMMER OF THE GREAT-GRANDMOTHER"

*M*y daughter lost her new shoes yesterday and, like any other mother, I was filled with righteous anger. I remembered the gloves, the pens, the rulers, the lacrosse boots, the three sweaters, the numberless hairbands, the hamster, the books, the nighties, the two watches, the tennis racket, the lip salves, the riding crops (gloves, hat), the anoraks, the wellington boots and the five swimming costumes.

"A whole family could be kitted out with your losings!" I cried. "I know," she said, looking sad. "I really liked those shoes, too."

... Life-enhancing rage slips... from my grip as I review the child's day and how she is expected to manipulate her possessions from 7.30 a.m. to five or six in the evening. ... Is it surprising that one pair of shoes has slipped through her fingers?

"Never mind about your new shoes, darling. You'll have grown out of them in six months and till then, you can wear jodhpur boots."

She smiles sweetly. "That's cool. You couldn't spare a minute to look for them?"

RACHEL BILLINGTON,
FROM "THE FAMILY TREE"

With girls, everything looks great on the surface. But beware of drawers that won't open. They contain a three-month supply of dirty underwear, unwashed hose, and rubber bands with blobs of hair in them.

ERMA BOMBECK

For all the time, very quietly, they are changing.

Before long, you are waving goodbye to them at the school gates.

A moment more and you have a teenager on your hands.

A flicker of time and they are leaving home – an independent woman.

But holding within them always the little children that they once were. Not just the memories of happiness and fears – of buttercup meadows, the grasses high above their heads, of secret places in the garden, of being lost – and found, of Christmas mornings.

But all those times beyond recall, when the world was very new and there was everything to learn.

We have to let go their hands.

But the joys we knew before, remembered or lost, are part of us all forever.

PAMELA DUGDALE

It will be gone before you know it.
The fingerprints on the wall appear
higher and higher.
Then suddenly they disappear.

DOROTHY EVSLIN, b. 1923

Arthur always had his arms around [his daughter] Camera. When he talked about her, his face would light up like stars in the sky. He showed more feeling for his daughter than I had seen him show his whole life.

HORACE ASHE, UNCLE OF ARTHUR ASHE

Dad has long and earnest conversations with his baby daughter.

He tells her she is noisy, undisciplined and manipulative —

and she will be sent back if she doesn't pull herself together.

And the baby smiles complacently.

She has him exactly where she wants him.

PAM BROWN, b.1928

I could look at my daughter and see the very image

I would like to have been able to hold of myself:

pretty, smart, and with a certain wisdom beyond her years.

I could discuss my ideas with her and she would be

admiring. I could consult with her about problems

I was having with "the kids" (her only slightly younger

brother and sister) and she would be supportive.

It was not as if I was without a partner in life; I'd lived

with Lowell for some time. Nevertheless, it was my daughter

who often seemed most meaningful in my struggle for my

lost Self. She was my little Echo, my "mirror," the answer

to a mother's dreams.

COLETTE DOWLING,
FROM "PERFECT WOMEN"

Melinda is a knockout. I never thought at my age I could knock off anything as brilliant and beautiful as she is. She is quite spoiled. Yesterday she threw quite a tantrum while out shopping because I wouldn't let her handle the wheel of the car. I tried to explain to her in small words that the police disapprove of babies fifteen months old driving Cadillacs, but she was furious....

GROUCHO MARX,
FROM A LETTER TO HIS DAUGHTER, MIRIAM, IN "LOVE, GROUCHO"

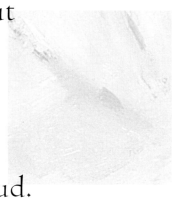

A tiny daughter
        seems like a dolly to dress — but
dolls do not vomit,
            poo, dribble —
or apply liberal quantities
            of paint and mud.

PAMELA DUGDALE

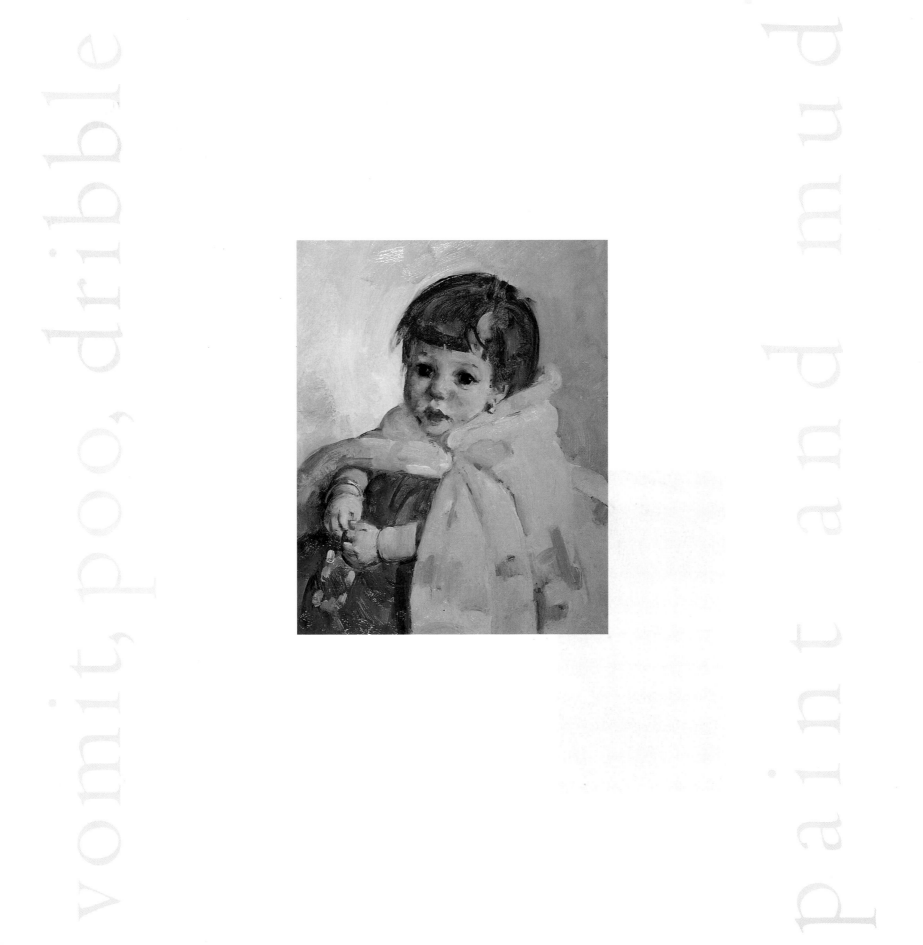

vomit, poo, dribble

paint and mud

... my darling girl
Sleeps and smiles and laughs, her face
So full of curiosity and magic
That I know the world was
Made in her honour.
She looks around her and as she looks
She renews all she sees.
The leaves rustle excitedly,
The curtains dance by the window,
The shadow moves beside her as
She turns and she turns and she turns,
Ocean eyes,
Taking it all in.

SALLY EMERSON,
FROM "BACK TO WORK"

Thank you for remembering

my stories, loving my made-up

games in the backyard and saying

all your friends loved the birthday

parties I over-organised!

LYNN MCLEAN

Thank you for an excuse to make home-made
jam and bake birthday cakes...
for bringing back fun to all our lives.

Thanks for all the cards — hand drawn
or by Renoir. For all the parcels — knobbly
or beribboned. For all the hurried kisses —
smelling of chocolate or Chanel.
For remembering.

PAM BROWN, b.1928

As a parent, I am going through a syndrome. It's called Joan of Arc, which means I am sick and tired of being treated like a dog with mouse breath. I'm sick of scrubbing and washing, running and fetching, scrimping and sewing, hauling and cooking only to have them say four words to me all year: Wait in the car. Last summer, I drove my daughter and son to the swimming pool. As my daughter and I prepared to emerge from the bathhouse, my daughter stopped.

"Where are you going?"

"Whatya mean where am I going? I am in a bathing suit. Am I dressed for a flu shot?"

"You go first," she commanded.

"Why, aren't they friendly?"

"Mom, no one goes to a swimming pool and sits with their mother."

"It's the bathing suit, isn't it?" I asked. "I should have shortened the sleeves."

"It's not the suit," she sighed.

"The varicose veins then. You're ashamed of my legs."

"The bathrobe covers them," she answered.

"What then?"

"It's just that the first thing you always do when you get inside is go in the water."

"I'd feel ridiculous swimming without it," I snapped. "What are you supposed to do at a swimming pool?"

"Other people's mothers don't go in the water."

..."Look," she said flatly, "I'm going to sit with some of my friends."

"Wonderful," I said. "When I am ready to go I"ll flash my compact mirror into the sun and spit three times into the wading pool."

... It must have been several hours before I felt a shadow over my towel. It was my two teen-agers.

"Hey, Mom, we want to get something cold to drink. Where's the money?" I brought myself up to one elbow, pulled my dark glasses down to the bridge of my nose and scrutinized them coolly, without recognition. "Whatsa matter, kids, lose your mother?" I said crisply and returned to my sun bathing.

That's one for St. Joan.

ERMA BOMBECK AND BIL KEENE,
FROM "JUST WAIT TILL YOU HAVE
CHILDREN OF YOUR OWN!"

's

thers

go

the

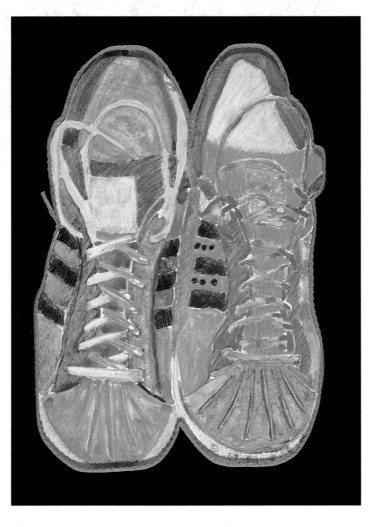

water"

A good daughter is like a good piece of writing:
candid, lyrical, graceful, moving, alive.
I have seen a young girl walk across a room,
intent on her intense errand, and it was like seeing
a voice become visible, as if not her tongue but her
motion said, "I will do this for my life."

PAUL ENGLE

Some people feel sorry for me and say I don't get out enough. There is absolutely no reason to feel sorry for me! How can they feel sorry for someone that has such a precious gift? I am so blessed by your presence in my life. Never before had I known a love as true, unconditional, and innocent.

JENNIFER, TO HER DAUGHTER KALLYSTA, FROM "LETTERS TO OUR DAUGHTERS"

... as she grew older she began to favour me, and nothing gave me more delight than her evident preference. I suppose I had not really expected her to dislike and resent me from birth, though I was quite prepared for resentment to follow later on, but I certainly had not anticipated such wreathing, dazzling gaiety of affection from her whenever I happened to catch her eye.

MARGARET DRABBLE, b.1939,
FROM "THE MILLSTONE"

IT SEEMS THAT WHENEVER I HAVE BEEN UPSET

OR ANNOYED WITH STEVE OR SAM,

LESLIE'S THE ONE I HAVE UNLOADED ON —

MY BOUNCING BOARD, MY LEVELER.

AN AWFUL BURDEN TO HAVE PLACED ON HER.

I APOLOGIZE TO YOU PUBLICLY,

MY DARLING DAUGHTER.

IT COMES FROM NOT HAVING A SIGNIFICANT

OR EVEN AN INSIGNIFICANT OTHER

TO TELL MY TROUBLES TO.

LAUREN BACALL,
b . 1 9 2 4

I recall a time in my life during which
I was in severe emotional pain.
One morning I woke up to find my
thirteen-year-old daughter sleeping on the floor
beside my bed. When I questioned her about this
she quietly told me that she wanted to be near me
because she knew I was hurting, but she didn't
want to risk disturbing my sleep.
The memory of this thoughtful expression
of her love and concern still brings tears of gratitude
eighteen years later.

BARBARA THOMAS

My Darling Stephanie,

I was asked to write about our relationship... but when I tried to just write about us, it became too emotional. Then I decided to try writing it all out in a letter to you.

It would be so easy to sum us up with a simple "I love you and you love me" because that is, after all, the case of this life we share. But it leaves so much unsaid.

It doesn't describe the pain we've felt or the acceptance we've had to make. Not over the fact that you're retarded, but pain because for some reason God must have felt there was more we needed to deal with. Big deal, you learn slower, and some things like calculus and understanding why Halley's Comet appears so seldom will never be possible for you. Such are the trade-offs in life. No matter how hard I try, I cannot make sense out of the pain and fear your many recent illnesses have caused you. I see the pain and another part of my heart dies and is replaced by an ache that remains — nothing takes it away, not even the incredible joy you bring me.

I've tried so hard to always be honest with you. But there are times when I feel like I'm cheating you. You ask me, "Why did I have to have so many strokes? Why don't my seizures stop? Why doesn't the pain go away?" I can only answer, "I don't know." I would give my life to make it all better, honey, but I can't. I can only promise to be there for you always. Whatever happens, we'll deal with it together.

... Don't misunderstand me. I'm not complaining. You've given me more love and joy than most mothers and daughters ever share. I'd do it all again just for the honor and the wonder of being your mother. You've taught me so much about self-growth, and you've shown me that no matter how tough or dark times seem to be, you'll always find a way to cope. I admire your strength so much; I draw all of mine from you.

I love you, Mom.

ANONYMOUS MOTHER,
FROM "A PORTRAIT OF
AMERICAN MOTHERS & DAUGHTERS"

I WISH THAT (IF EVER SHE SEES THIS) I COULD GIVE

HER [MY ELDEST DAUGHTER, MARIANNE] THE

SLIGHTEST IDEA OF THE LOVE AND THE HOPE

THAT IS BOUND UP IN HER. THE LOVE WHICH

PASSETH EVERY EARTHLY LOVE, AND THE HOPE

THAT HOWEVER WE MAY BE SEPARATED ON EARTH,

WE MAY... MEET AGAIN TO RENEW THE DEAR

AND TENDER TIE OF MOTHER AND DAUGHTER.

ELIZABETH GASKELL,
FROM "MY DIARY"

I miss
those days

I miss the red galoshes and the shiny quilted blue snowsuits marching along in a happy cadence; the yellow pajamas with the feet on them that snap up the front and were the costume after the bath. I miss the colorful illustrated notes my girls pinned on their bedroom doors with messages of love and lots of XOXOXOs. I miss our painting sessions, when we'd sit at the kitchen table with our huge pads of white paper and share a pot of Magic Markers and colored pencils....

I miss holding my little ones in my lap by the warm glow of a crackling fire reading all my favorite childhood books which they also cherished. I miss hunting for mica in the sand at the playground, doing somersaults on the lawn, decorating their rooms with them, helping them grow plants in their indoor window boxes, and helping each of them to create a secret place to go be alone.

I miss my girls taking turns over who would sit next to me at breakfast, lunch, and dinner. I miss our nature walks in the early spring, discovering the first forsythia and a host of daffodils smiling brightly in the warm, fragrant spring air. I miss the trips to the flower shop, the ice cream store, and the bakery. I miss hanging out in the library at the children's tables, sitting on brightly painted little chairs. I miss the beach days, the swim meets, the ribbons. I miss the train trips, the car rides, the buses, and the airplanes. I miss raking leaves and climbing the hill to the apple orchard to pick apples in October for making applesauce and pies together. I miss having the girls decorate the cheese platter when friends came over, and then serve the hors d'oeuvres to our guests. In their long, Laura Ashley flowered dresses and with shining clean hair, they glowed with pride in their family.

ALEXANDRA STODDARD,
FROM "MOTHERS: A CELEBRATION"

I used to love watching them together. He didn't know quite what to do with her - he would gaze at her with wonder in his eyes. She was delicate, she was a girl, so he would be delicate with her. He was a gentle man, not overly demonstrative, yet when he looked at his daughter you could see him melt. He became totally vulnerable.

LAUREN BACALL, b.1924, FROM "NOW"

He is totally transformed by his first daughter. There is a gentleness about him that even love never discovered. He holds her like a flower, like thinnest glass. He wonders at this new and lovely life, incredible in its perfection.

PAM BROWN, b.1928

her like a flower

Thank you for giving me back Pooh Bear and Ratty and Curdie and Milly-Molly-Mandy. Thank you for reminding me of stars and fallen leaves, winter beaches, summer woods. Thank you for tadpoles and slow-worms and spiders named Alfred.

PAM BROWN, b.1928

Your first swan.
Your first day by
the sea. Your first
walk through a
field of spring
flowers. The first
time you heard
and loved Chopin.
In sharing your
childhood
discoveries, I have
relived my own.

MARION C. GARRETTY,
b. 1917

*I*t doesn't make any difference how much money a father earns, his name is always Dad-Can-I; and he always wonders whether these little people were born to beg. I bought each of my five children everything up to a Rainbow Brite jacuzzi and still I kept hearing "Dad, can I get... Dad, can I go... Dad, can I buy...".

Like all other children, my five have one great talent: they are gifted beggars....

Sometimes, at three or four in the morning, I open the door to one of the children's bedrooms and watch the light softly fall across their little faces. And then I quietly kneel beside one of the beds and just look at the girl lying there because she is so beautiful. And because she is not begging. Kneeling there, I listen reverently to the sound of her breathing.

And then she wakes up and says, "Dad, can I...".

BILL COSBY

FROM "FATHERHOOD"

Things to worry about:
  Worry about courage
  Worry about cleanliness
  Worry about efficiency...
Things not to worry about:
  Don't worry about popular opinion
  Don't worry about dolls
  Don't worry about the past
  Don't worry about the future
  Don't worry about growing up
  Don't worry about anybody getting ahead of you
  Don't worry about triumph
  Don't worry about failure unless it comes
  through your own fault....

F. SCOTT FITZGERALD (1896-1940)

Never grow a wishbone, daughter,
where your backbone ought to be.

CLEMENTINE PADDLEFORD

My prayer is that you will learn

those characteristics that are worthy of possessing:

love, servanthood, forgiveness, honesty, sincerity...

I can only hope that I can be an example to you.

AMY, FROM "LETTERS TO OUR DAUGHTERS"

If you don't put your shoes on before I count fifteen then
we won't go to the woods to climb the chesnut
one

    But I can't find them

Two

    I can't

They're under the sofa **three**

    No

    O yes

Four five six

    Stop – they've got knots they've got knots

You should untie the laces when you take your

shoes off **seven**

    Will you do one shoe while I do the other then?

Eight but that would be cheating

    Please

All right

    It always...

Nine

    It always sticks – I'll use my teeth

Ten

    It won't it won't

    It has – look.

Eleven

    I'm not wearing any socks

Twelve

    Stop counting stop counting. Mum where
    are my socks mum

They're in your shoes. Where you left them.
    I didn't
Thirteen
    O they're inside out and upside down and
    bundled up
Fourteen
    Have you done the knot on the shoe
    you were...
Yes
Put it on the right foot
    But socks don't have right and wrong foot
The shoes silly
Fourteen and a half
    I am I am. Wait.
    Don't go to the woods without me
    Look that's one shoe already
Fourteen and threequarters
    There
You haven't tied the bows yet
    We could do them on the way there
No we won't **fourteen and seven eights**
    Help me then
    You know I'm not fast at bows
Fourteen and fifteen sixteeeenths
    A single bow is all right isn't it
Fifteen we're off
    See I did it.
    Didn't I?

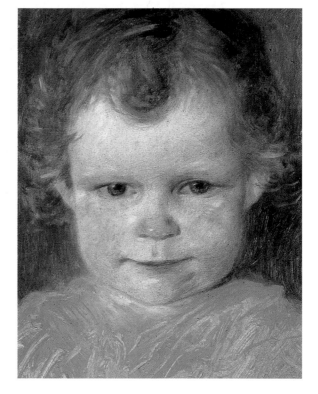

M I C H A E L   R O S E N

Take a sixteen-year-old for a walk in the country

and she can still bound like the lambs in the field.

Take her to the seaside and she will still chase the waves

in and out up to her waist.

She still likes snowballing, climbing up hay bales,

rolling down grassy slopes, lying on the lawn

and watching the clouds turn into fierce animals.

RACHEL BILLINGTON, FROM "THE GREAT UMBILICAL"

You must be free to take a path

Whose end I feel no need to know,

So you can go without regret

Away from this familiar land,

Leaving your kiss upon my hair

And all the future in your hands.

MARGARET MEAD (1901-1978),
FOR HER DAUGHTER CATHY, FROM "BLACKBERRY WINTER"

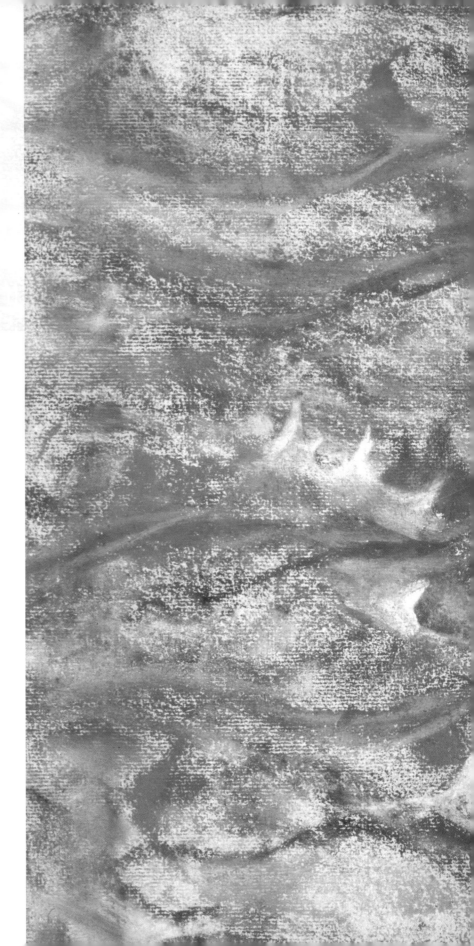

My daughter is now playing out her closing scenes for me. The other evening I watched her dancing at home to the gramophone — something she'd done since she was small, but never quite like this. I watched a swirling figure, wrapped in a solitary glow, dancing in loose-limbed controlled abandon; dancing for her reflection in the mirror, for a glance from me; but also for that other one, unknown and unguessed at yet, for whom these spells were cast, for that future-one who must in time replace me.

And watching her dancing there in that brief and questioning solitude of her body, I felt all the sad enchantment of seeing something about to take wing. That as soon as the limbs were tested and proved, the will found to be strong enough, she would be risen and away and gone from me at last, leaving behind the dropped dolls, the circling goldfish, the empty hamster cage, and the horse in the field with its turned raised head.

LAURIE LEE (1914-1977),
FROM "TWO WOMEN"

daughters are the thing

Fame is rot, daughters are the thing.

J.M. BARRIE,

FROM "DEAR BRUTUS"

I have a beautiful daughter,
golden like a flower, my beloved Cleis,
for her, in her place, I would not accept
the whole of Lydia...

SAPPHO

*In the lottery of my life,
my daughter is the six numbers —
and the bonus.*

UNKNOWN AUTHOR,

FROM "COSMOPOLITAN", MARCH 1997

To love a daughter can be difficult at times. They are inclined to shear off the beautiful hair that you have cherished. To dye the stubble magenta. To opt for wearing rags – or worse. To give up the course they made you wheedle the headteacher into allowing. To attach themselves to strange groups and causes. And stranger boyfriends. To frighten you at frequent intervals. To veer between ecstasy and misery. To drop bombshells. They are trying lives on for size. The daughter you know and love is still there.

PAM BROWN, b. 1928

When a girl hits thirteen, you can just
watch her lose her mind.
Luckily, she gets it back;
but during the time that it's misplaced,
you can lose your own.

BILL COSBY

Many a father wishes he were
strong enough to tear
a telephone book in two -
especially if he has a teenage daughter.

GUY LOMABARDO

No daughter decides to
leave any organization
until her parents have
bought all the required kit.

CHARLOTTE GRAY,
b. 1937

A teenage daughter is easier to love
in retrospect.

JAN DU PLESSIS

One tiny tug will have me dropping

any masterpiece on which I am engaged —

you are, above everything,

the heartbeat of my life.

PAMELA DUGDALE

I have always told all of you
that you can do anything you put your mind to
and that Mom and Dad will give you
all the support, love, advice, and help
you need to reach your goal.

SABRINA,
TO HER DAUGHTERS MARIAH, BEVERLEY & DIEDRE,
FROM "LETTERS TO OUR DAUGHTERS"

If you could prove you wanted to do something very badly — rock climbing,

scuba diving, growing begonias, breeding fish — and were prepared to work at

it — a dad would back you all the way. And if the enthusiasm faded, he would

not fuss — but just say, "All experience comes in handy, one day or another."

PETER GRAY, b.1928

After you were born, I kept doing my work as usual,
but now there was even more reason for graduating.
It wasn't for me anymore, it was for you.
I would do anything and everything to make sure
that you had the best life possible.
I strongly believe in the importance of a good education
and that I must set strong examples for you.
I want you to be the very best you can be,
and I think that being the best I can be
is the first step for you.

JENNIFER, TO HER DAUGHTER KALLYSTA,
FROM "LETTERS TO OUR DAUGHTERS"

And then, there she was, curled up in a cot next to me,
an easy, contented, restful baby, who would grow into a relaxed,
merry little girl, belying the trauma of her journey here.
But oh how vulnerable. How I have prayed that no biting,
stinging word of mine, no inadvertent word of bitterness or
sarcasm, jealousy or malice, would poison or diminish
the joyous, loving, laughing gift I have held in my cupped hands
for the last eleven years. An awesome responsibility
for a mother, to lead a daughter into truth.

MICHELE GUINNESS,
FROM "TAPESTRY OF VOICES"

the best I can be

$\mathcal{D}$aughters are more precious

than gold.

More precious

than any inanimate thing,

however beautiful.

More precious

than one's dreams,

however glorious....

They are its hope.

And yours to love.

MARION C. GARRETTY

The teenage girl has won herself a reputation for intractability.... Yet there is another side to the story, not often told but experienced by many mothers. So I make no apology for singing a few glad tidings on the loving, happy aspects of the young... girl growing into womanhood....

They come mostly from the girl's freshness, her curiosity, her openness, her irresponsibility, her exuberance (despite all pressures), her affection, her loyalty, her sympathy, her gentleness, her wide-eyed enjoyment of things that her mother has started to take for granted or lost interest in altogether.

RACHEL BILLINGTON,

FROM "THE GREAT UMBILICAL"

I call my daughter "princess"

because every movement and gesture she makes,

the harmony in her voice, her smile, her pranks,

her ingenuity — all these indicate a royal character.

Moreover she is despotic and holds firmly to her own ideas,

without anyone being able to change or modify

them — but sweet indeed is her despotism and her

absolute judgment.

KAHLIL GIBRAN
(1 8 8 3 – 1 9 3 1)

My daughter is now six years old.

This, to me, is much more a miracle

than having three books on the bestseller

list at the same time.

MICHAEL CRICHTON

Your thin little body is as close to life

as I have come.

You who are life itself when I touch you and you become

heavy and warm and lean against me. When you pat my

cheek and say: "Little Mamma", and understand more

than I realise.

When you say that I must not be sad, because you

are there.

When you make life richer, just by being.

Dear Linn....

A contact which is without words and without touch.

I stand by the window and see you.... You have thoughts

and adventures I shall never share. I stand and look at

you and am closer to you than anything else I know about.

You are a part of me which is completely free.

And I watch you, wishing I had the time to follow you

more closely. See how your freedom lives in you.

LIV ULLMANN,

FROM "CHANGING"

BUT I DID KISS YOU IN THE NIGHT

AND CHASED AWAY YOUR NIGHTMARES;

AND I MADE UP STORIES AND SONGS

THAT MADE YOU LAUGH FULL AND STRONG,

AND MOST TIMES, I WAS THERE FOR YOU

AND RECOGNIZED, MOST CLEARLY

THAT FACING YOU IS FACING ME.

AND I ENCOURAGED YOU TO CLAIM YOUR LIFE

AND FIGHT LIKE HELL FOR YOUR RIGHT TO BE;

AND THE BEST GIFT THAT I COULD EVER GIVE TO YOU

WAS TO SAY "YES" TO YOUR DREAMS

THAT WERE NOT MY OWN.

MARGARET SLOAN-HUNTER, FROM "PASSING"

dreams

Dear Daughter. Take my love with you now and into the time that I will never know. It is as much a part of you as breath. Or your identity.

CHARLOTTE GRAY, b. 1937

As we move off into the future, two separate

women each struggling to complete herself,

I know that we will reach out to each other.

In my strength I can be a tree for you to lean

against. In my weakness, I will need your hand.

RITA FREEDMAN

Know that I am your greatest ally and fan. I will
continue to applaud at your victories and walk with
you through trials and mistakes. I look in your faces
and am proud of who we are — who you are as a
result of being my daughters — and even more, proud
of who I am because of the honor and privilege of
being your mother.

MOLLY, TO HER DAUGHTERS HALEY AND LAUREN

As I start the twilight years of my life, I try to look back
and figure out what it was all about. I'm still not sure what
is meant by good fortune and success. I know fame and power
are for the birds. But then life suddenly comes into focus for me.
And, ah, there stand my kids. I love them.

LEE IACOCCA,
FROM "TALKING STRAIGHT"

Having been fashioned from me, all you do —
despite your freedom —
must affect me too.
And so when we're apart
I will always long for news from you.

MAYA V. PATEL, b.1943

I thought about Leslie.... I don't see enough of her.... It's either too late

for her to call me when her day ends or too early for me to call her

when mine does. I miss her, miss our lengthy conversations.

I miss being able to share time. Our approach to life is so different,

and she's so different from her brothers — it's good for me

to listen to her, hear her point of view. She has expanded my horizons,

she is my most natural resource.

LAUREN BACALL, b.1924,

FROM "NOW"

miss her

We are friends.
We have loads of fun together,
and our grooves continue to sew the years
into a beautiful tapestry.

ALEXANDRA STODDARD

Thank you, my dearest girl,
for telling me when your friend is in trouble,
even though there's nothing I can do to be of any help.
Thank you for newspaper articles you thought
might interest me. Thank you for the phone call
to tell me of a TV documentary that's just starting.
Thank you for birthday cards that are exactly right.
Thank you for asking me for recipes.
Thank you for giving me advice.
Thank you for letting me into your life.

PAMELA DUGDALE

Hyacinth Manning

Ruth, my love, you know only too well
my immense love for and pride in you.
When I see before me a confident young woman
and when others tell me what a beautiful daughter
I have, I am proud, but it is not because
I take any credit. I am proud and pleased
for you because you are your own person.
What you have and what you give to others
comes from inside you, and whatever it is,
it is very special....

MARIAN, TO HER DAUGHTER RUTH,
FROM "LETTERS TO OUR DAUGHTERS"

I'm proud of you
not for the things that came easily to you —
or that were part of you from the very beginning —
but for your slogging it out against the odds
and against your nature and spluttering
to the surface with your prize.

PAMELA DUGDALE

you are your

Dear Daughter.

You cost me a fortune in nappies and gripe water, shoes and skirts and hockey sticks. You broke my sleep, you broke my golfing trophy and you nearly broke my heart on several occasions. You were obstinate, noisy, rude, untidy, argumentative, disobedient, lazy — and you backed the car over my geraniums. You read the wrong books, studied the wrong subjects, got the wrong qualifications.

Your boyfriends have been near certifiable.

But you're wonderful.

And I love you.

Dad.

DR. PETER SPEARS

Thank you for wilting dandelions,

for twigs of lambstails,

for wet pebbles, for fluff-covered toffees,

for sticky kisses.

Thank you for loving me.

Some daughters give Cartier watches

and Cointreau.

Some daughters send shrubs,

sweaters and home-made jam.

The thing is — daughters know exactly

what one needs.

PAMELA DUGDALE

*S*he is yours to hold in your cupped hands, to guard and to guide. Give her your strength and wisdom and all the good that life can offer. Yours is a sacred trust. Never harm her with words that can bite and sting. Lead her into truth.

MICHELE GUINNESS, FROM "TAPESTRY OF VOICES"

I have not been a perfect mother,
but I have always cherished you,
guided you, believed in you, and
stood by you.
It is the promise I made at your births.
It is the promise I make to you
for the rest of my life.

KATHRYN, TO HER DAUGHTERS JENNA AND KRISTEN

When I'm not tranquil,

she will try to steady me.

My periods of loneliness,

she reassures me.

What a marvelous daughter

she is! Such humanity.

She has a sweetness

I don't have.

An understanding heart

I don't have.

A tranquillity.

... Everything that I dreamed of

for myself has happened

to Sophia.

I live in her image.

ROMILDA VILLANI,
FROM "SOPHIA: LIVING AND LOVING"

Sometimes when I'm feeling

particularly useless you give me

sound advice — which I once gave you.

It cheers me up no end.

Thanks for keeping an eye on me, love.

PAMELA DUGDALE

Thirty-four years of unbroken kindness,

of cloudless sunshine, of perpetual joy, of constant love. Thirty-four years

of happy smiles, of loving looks and gentle words, of generous deeds.

Thirty-four years, a flower, a palm, a star, a faultless child, a perfect

woman, wife, and mother.

ROBERT G. INGERSOLL
(1 8 3 3 - 1 8 9 9)
IN A BIRTHDAY NOTE TO HIS DAUGHTER, EVA

We played, we sang, we danced wildly. And we wandered quietly by the sea. I will always remember these days in summer – they are in my very being. You were, you are my daughter. My daughter, my joy.

HELEN THOMSON, b.1943

ACKNOWLEDGEMENTS

Exley Publications is very grateful to the individuals and organizations who have granted permission to reproduce their pictures. Whilst all reasonable efforts have been made to clear copyright and acknowledge sources and artists, Exley Publications would be happy to hear from any copyright holder who may have been omitted.
A very special thank you to the following for contributing so much to the visual beauty and the sourcing of the pictures in this book: AISA, Archiv für Kunst, Art Resource, Artworks, Charlotte Aston, Bridgeman Art Library, Bulloz, Chris Beetles Gallery, Christie's Images, James Clift, Edimedia, Exley Photographic Library, Fine Art Photographic Library Ltd, Giraudon, Alex Goldberg, Dora Goldberg, Image Select International, Martin Kerr, Claire Lipscomb, Richard Mason, Scala, Superstock.

PICTURE ACKNOWLEDGEMENTS

Cover, endpapers, half title, title page: **Girl in a Poppyfield**, *Dora Hitz (1856-1924)*, Museum der Bildenden Künste, Leipzig.

Page 4: **Blonde-haired Girl**, © 1998 *Martha Walter (1875-1976)*, David David Gallery, Philadelphia.

Page 7: **Au Bord du Lac**, *Berthe Morisot (1841-1895)*, Marmottan Museum.

Page 8: **Girl Holding Magazine**, © 1998 *Martha Walter (1875-1976)*, David David Gallery, Philadelphia.

Page 10: **Three Ages of Woman** (detail), *Gustav Klimt (1862-1918)*, Gallery of Modern Art, Rome (opposite Jane-Louise Middleton quotation).

Page 12: **A Good Book**, © 1998 *Walter Firle (1859-1929)*.

Page 15: **Der Stammhalter**, © 1998 *L. A. Tessier*.

Page 16: **Perdita "Blossom Speed You Well" Winters Tale**, *Amelia Bauerle* d.1916.

Page 17: **Kept In** (detail), © 1998 *John Henry Henshall (1856-1928)*, Christopher Wood Gallery, London.

Page 18: **Her First Christmas**, © 1998 *Robert Gemmell Hutchinson (1855-1936)*, Private Collection.

Page 20: **At the end of October/Nîmes**, *Duez*, Musée des Beaux-Arts (opposite Bette Davis quotation).

Page 23: *Ferdinand Delacroix (1798-1863)*.

Pages 24/25: **Cliff Steps, Minsmere Cliffs, Suffolk**, © 1998 *Charles Neal*.

Page 26: **Baby with Beads**, © 1998 *Martha Walter (1875-1976)*, David David Gallery, Philadelphia.

Page 29: **Claude Renoir Playing**, *Pierre Auguste Renoir (1841-1919)*, Musée de L'Orangerie, Paris (opposite Virginia Woolf quotation).

Page 30: **The Butcher's Shop**, © 1998 *Robert Medley*, Private Collection.

Page 32: **In the Hawthorn Hedge**, *Carl Larsson (1855-1919)*, Christies, London.

Page 35: **The Young Mother and Child**, *Muyden*, Petit Palais, Paris.

Page 37: **Picasso's Eiffel Tower Journey**, © 1998 *Tsing-Fang Chen*, Lucia Gallery, New York (opposite Susan Hill quotation).

Pages 38/39: **Sloe Blossom**, © 1998 *William Stewart Macgeorge (1861-1931)*, Smith Art Gallery and Museum, Stirling.

Page 40: **In the Artist's Studio**, *Alexander Rossi (1870-1903)*, Whitford and Hughes, London.

Page 42: **A Visiting Performance of the Soviet State Circus in East Germany**, © 1998 *Hartmut Genz*.

Page 45: **Baby**, *Porfini Krylov*, Tretiakov Gallery, Moscow.

Page 46: **Nursing the Baby**, © 1998 *Lilla Cabot Perry (1848-1933)*, David David Gallery, Philadelphia.

Page 48: **Lost Child**, *Arthur Hughes (1830-1915)*.

Page 50: **The Kiss**, *W. Lee Hankey* (opposite J.B. Griffiths quotation).

Pages 52/53: **Study of the Countryside at Florence**, *A. Faldi*, Gallery of Modern Art.

Page 55: **Feeding Time**, © 1998 *Martha Walter (1875-1976)*, David David Gallery, Philadelphia.

Page 56: **The Foundling**, *Frederick Cayley Robinson (1862-1927)*, Leamington Spa Museum and Art Gallery, England.

Page 58: **Child With Whip**, 1885, *Pierre Auguste Renoir (1841-1919)*, Hermitage Museum, St Petersburg (opposite Madeleine L'Engle quotation).

Pages 60/61: **Bella's Room**, © 1998 *Timothy Easton*, (living artist) Private Collection.

Page 62: **Sun and Moon Flowers**, *George Dunlop Leslie (1835-1921)*, Guildhall Art Gallery, Corporation of London.

Page 64: **Feeding Time**, © 1998 *T. Gaponenko*, Tretiakov Gallery, Moscow.

Page 66: **The Pastor's Daughter**, © 1998 *Chuikov*, Tretiakov Gallery, Moscow.

Page 69: **Girl in Pink Cape**, © 1998 *Martha Walter (1875-1976)*, David David Gallery, Philadelphia.

Pages 70/71: **Meadow, Perrotts Brook, Gloucestershire**, © 1998 *Charles Neal*.

Page 72: © 1998 *Peter Fiore*, Private Collection.

Page 75: **Shoe series #2**, © 1998 *Marilee Whitehouse-Holm*, Private Collection.

Pages 76/77: © 1998 *Marina Kamina*, Private Collection.

Page 79: **Exodus – 1893**, *Boll*, Petit Palais, Paris.

Page 81: **Interior (1901)**, *Georg-Nicolaj Achen*, Musée D'Orsay, Paris.

Page 83: **Apparition in Blue Pastel**, © 1998 *Lucien Levy Dhurmer (1865-1953)*.

Page 85: **Portrait of Helen Gow**, *Alexander Mann, (1853-1908)*, Private Collection (opposite Elizabeth Gaskell quotation).

Page 87: **A Heavy Burden**, *Arthur Hacker (1858-1919)*, Private Collection.

Pages 88/89: **Provencal Spring**, © 1998 *Henry Herbert La Thangue (1859-1929)*, Bradford Art Galleries and Museums.

Page 90: **Portrait of Mika Morozov**, *Serov Valentin (1865-1911)* Tretiakov Gallery, Moscow.

Page 93: **Children Walking**, *Timoleon Marie Lobrichom (1831-1914)*, Roy Miles Gallery, London.

Page 95: **Child's Head**, *Hans Am Ende (1864-1918)* (opposite Michael Rosen poem).

Page 97: **Portrait of a dark-haired girl**, *Paul Friedrich Meyerheim (1842-1915)*, Phillips, The International Fine Art Auctioneers.

Pages 98/99: **Gust of Wind**, © 1998 *Lucien Levy-Dhurmer (1865-1953)*, Private Collection.

Page 100: **Maternal Love**, © 1998 *Vicenzo Trolli (1960-1942)*, Josef Mensing Gallery, Hamm-Rhynern (opposite Sappho quotation).

Page 102: **Winter Sunshine**, © 1998 *Gwendolyn Grant (1878-1940)*, Private Collection.

Page 104: **Girl Playing a Violin**, © 1998 *Fritz Freitag (1915-1977)*.

Page 106: **A Family Group**, *Sir Lawrence Alma-Tadema (1836-1912)*, Royal Academy of Art, London.

Page 109: **The Young Shepherdess**, *William-Adolphe Bougereau (1825-1905)*, San Diego Museum of Art.

Page 111: **Heads**, *Artist Unknown* (French), David David Gallery, Philadelphia.

Page 112: **Girl with a Toy Parrot**, © 1998 *Harold Harvey (1874-1941)*, Waterhouse and Dodd, London.

Page 115: **The Mischievous Girl**, © 1998 *Benito Rebolledo Correa (1880-1964)*, Kactus Foto, Santiago.

Page 117: **Butterfly**, © 1998 *Ilja Repin (1844-1930)*, Tretiakov Gallery, Moscow (opposite Liv Ullmann quotation).

Page 119: **Julia Payne and her son Ivan**, © 1998 *Julius Gari Melchers (1860-1932)*.

Page 120: **In the Yellow Light**, *James Carroll Beckwith (1852-1917)*.

Page 123: **Young Woman Arranging Her Hair**, *J. Alexander*.

Page 124: **The Window on Pomaio**, *Vito d'Ancona*, Private Collection (opposite Maya Patel & Lauren Bacall quotations).

Page 127: **Wedding – series 1**, © 1998 *Hyacinth Manning*.

Page 129: **Woman's Face by the Forest**, *Tihamer von Margitay*.

Page 131: **Blonde Girl Combing Her Hair**, *Pierre Auguste Renoir (1841-1919)*, Metropolitan Museum of Art, New York.

Page 133: **Girl with a Silver Fish**, © 1998 *William Robert Symonds (1851-1934)*, Ipswich Borough Council Museums and Galleries.

Page 134: **Mother and Child**, © 1998 *Angelito Antonio*.

Page 136: **Heads**, *Artist Unknown* (French), David David Gallery, Philadelphia.

Page 138: **Portrait of Lady Ljubatovic**, © 1998 *Korovin Konstantin (1861-1939)*, Museo Statale Russo, Leningrad.

Pages 140/141: **The Maiden Voyage**, © 1998 *Joseph Farquharson (1847-1935)*.

The publishers are grateful for permission to reproduce copyright material. Whilst every reasonable effort has been made to trace copyright holders, the publishers would be pleased to hear from any not here acknowledged.

LAUREN BACALL: from *Now* by Lauren Bacall, © 1994, published by Hutchinson. Reprinted by permission of Random House UK Ltd.

ALAN BECK: from *What is a Girl?* published by the New England Life Insurance Co., USA.

RACHEL BILLINGTON: from *The Great Umbilical* by Rachel Billington, published by Hutchinson, and *The Family Year* by Rachel Billington published by Macmillan. Reprinted by permission of David Higham Associates.

ERMA BOMBECK: from *Just Wait Till You Have Children Of Your Own* by Erma Bombeck. © 1971 Erma Bombeck and Bill Keane. Used by permission of Doubleday, a division of Bantam Doubleday Dell Publishing Group.

JOHN CIARDI: *Someone's Face* © The Ciardi Family Publishing Trust.

BILL COSBY: from *Fatherhood* © 1986 William H. Cosby Jr, published by Bantam Books.

MARGARET DRABBLE: from *The Millstone* by Margaret Drabble, published by Wiedenfeld and Nicholson.

SALLY EMERSON: From "Back to Work" from *Occasional Poets* published by Viking Penguin, 1986. Reprinted by permission of Curtis Brown Ltd.

KAHLIL GIBRAN: From *Gibran Love Letters* published by One World © S.B. Bushrui and Salma Haffer al-Kuzberi. Reprinted by permission of Alfred A. Knopf Inc.

MICHELE GUINNESS: from *Tapestry of Voices* published by Triangle/SPCK, 1993. © 1993 Michele Guinness, reprinted with permission of SPCK.

SUSAN HILL: from *Family* by Susan Hill, published by Michael Joseph, 1989. Reprinted with permission from Penguin Books Ltd.

LEE IACOCCA: from *Talking Straight* © 1988 by Lee Iacocca. Reprinted by permission of Bantam, a division of Bantam Doubleday Dell Publishing Group, Inc.

BRIAN JONES: from "You Being Born" from *Spitfire on the Northern Line* by Brian Jones, published by Bodley Head, reprinted by permission of Random House UK, Ltd.

LAURIE LEE: from *Two Women* by Laurie Lee, © 1983 Laurie Lee. Reprinted by permission of Penguin Books Ltd. From *I Can't Stay Long* published by Andre Deutsch 1975 reprinted by permission of Penguin Books Ltd. & Peters, Fraser & Dunlop Group Ltd.

MADELEINE L'ENGLE: from *The Summer of the Great-Grandmother*. This usage granted by permission copyright 1974 by Crosswicks Ltd.

LETTERS TO OUR DAUGHTERS: Extracts from *Letters to our Daughters*, © 1997 Kristine Van Raden and Molly Davis, published by Beyond Words Publishing Inc. ISBN 1-800-284-9673.

SUE LIMB: from *Love, Forty* published by Corgi Books 1988, a division of Transworld Publishers Ltd. Reprinted by permission of The Peters, Fraser and Dunlop Group Ltd on behalf of Sue Limb.

GROUCHO MARX: from *Love, Groucho* published by Faber and Faber. © 1992 Miriam Marx Allen.

LINDA GRAY SEXTON: from *Points of Light*, published by Michael Joseph 1988. © Linda Gray Sexton.

MARGARET SLOAN-HUNTER: from "Passing", from *A Portrait of American Mothers and Daughters,* published by NewSage Press, 1987.

HARRY STEIN: from *Esquire* October 1981. © 1981 Harry Stein.

ALEXANDRA STODDARD: from *Mothers: A Celebration* published by William Morrow & Co Ltd. © 1996 Alexandra Stoddard.

LIV ULLMAN: from *Changing*, published by Wiedenfeld & Nicholson, 1977. © 1976, 1977 Liv Ullman.

VIRGINIA WOOLF: from *A Writer's Diary* published by Hogarth Press. Reprinted with permission of Random House UK Ltd, on behalf of the Executors of the Virginia Woolf Estate and Harcourt Brace and Co.

HELEN EXLEY, the anthologist who created *My Daughter, my joy...,* is an editor of many years standing, and has many books to her credit, but this book is special. "I myself am a very loved daughter. My mother means everything to me, and working with the sensitive words and pictures for this collection has been a moving experience," she says.

Helen Exley's books have sold over twenty million copies, and the secret of her success, she says, is simple. "I try to create beautiful giftbooks that put into words the things that people often find so hard to say. With my researchers and designers I have access to the whole world of art and literature. I am spoilt for choice with the greatest paintings and the greatest words ever written. My job is simply to conceive a presentation, a design and a title of a book, and then to choose and arrange the quotations and illustrations in a way that expresses people's real inner feelings, and that says, in one way or another, "Thanks for everything. You mean so much to me".

"It's a life's work, and I find it very, very fulfilling," Helen says. "Time after time people tell me just how important the books have been in building bonds and helping them to express their deepest thoughts. People really seem to appreciate the books, and that's my ultimate satisfaction, and why I love the job."

Helen is C.E.O. of her own publishing company.